FREE Study Skills Videos,

Dear Customer,

Thank you for your purchase from Mometrix! We consider it an honor and a privilege that you have purchased our product and we want to ensure your satisfaction.

As part of our ongoing effort to meet the needs of test takers, we have developed a set of Study Skills Videos that we would like to give you for FREE. These videos cover our *best practices* for getting ready for your exam, from how to use our study materials to how to best prepare for the day of the test.

All that we ask is that you email us with feedback that would describe your experience so far with our product. Good, bad, or indifferent, we want to know what you think!

To get your FREE Study Skills Videos, you can use the **QR code** below, or send us an **email** at studyvideos@mometrix.com with *FREE VIDEOS* in the subject line and the following information in the body of the email:

- The name of the product you purchased.
- Your product rating on a scale of 1-5, with 5 being the highest rating.
- Your feedback. It can be long, short, or anything in between. We just want to know your impressions and experience so far with our product. (Good feedback might include how our study material met your needs and ways we might be able to make it even better. You could highlight features that you found helpful or features that you think we should add.)

If you have any questions or concerns, please don't hesitate to contact me directly.

Thanks again!

Sincerely,

Jay Willis
Vice President
jay.willis@mometrix.com
1-800-673-8175

US Citizenship Test Study Guide 2023 and 2024

USCIS Naturalization Civics Exam Secrets Book

Complete Practice Question List

Detailed Answer Explanations

3rd Edition

Written and edited by the Mometrix Adult Education Test Team

Printed in the United States of America

This paper meets the requirements of ANSI/NISO Z39.48-1992 (Permanence of Paper).

Mometrix offers volume discount pricing to institutions. For more information or a price quote, please contact our sales department at sales@mometrix.com or 888-248-1219.

Mometrix Media LLC is not affiliated with or endorsed by any official testing organization. All organizational and test names are trademarks of their respective owners.

ISBN 13: 978-1-5167-2233-4
ISBN 10: 1-5167-2233-7

DEAR FUTURE EXAM SUCCESS STORY

First of all, **THANK YOU** for purchasing Mometrix study materials!

Second, congratulations! You are one of the few determined test-takers who are committed to doing whatever it takes to excel on your exam. **You have come to the right place.** We developed these study materials with one goal in mind: to deliver you the information you need in a format that's concise and easy to use.

In addition to optimizing your guide for the content of the test, we've outlined our recommended steps for breaking down the preparation process into small, attainable goals so you can make sure you stay on track.

We've also analyzed the entire test-taking process, identifying the most common pitfalls and showing how you can overcome them and be ready for any curveball the test throws you.

Standardized testing is one of the biggest obstacles on your road to success, which only increases the importance of doing well in the high-pressure, high-stakes environment of test day. Your results on this test could have a significant impact on your future, and this guide provides the information and practical advice to help you achieve your full potential on test day.

Your success is our success

We would love to hear from you! If you would like to share the story of your exam success or if you have any questions or comments in regard to our products, please contact us at **800-673-8175** or **support@mometrix.com**.

Thanks again for your business and we wish you continued success!

Sincerely,
The Mometrix Test Preparation Team

TABLE OF CONTENTS

Introduction

Thank you for purchasing this resource! You have made the choice to prepare yourself for a test that could have a huge impact on your future, and this guide is designed to help you be fully ready for test day.

In this guide, we will not only show you **every question** that you might be asked on the test, but we will also give you the background knowledge so you will understand the answers to these questions and why they are important.

If you struggle with **test anxiety**, we strongly encourage you to check out our recommendations for how you can overcome it. Test anxiety is a formidable foe, but it can be beaten, and we want to make sure you have the tools you need to defeat it.

Test Format

There are two parts to the citizenship test: the **English test** and the **civics test**.

The English test will require you to show that you are able to speak, read, and write English well enough to fulfill your duties as a US citizen:

- The interviewer will assess your ability to **speak** English during the eligibility interview.
- To test your **reading** ability, you will be given up to three sentences in English, and you must successfully read aloud at least one of the three sentences in order to pass.
- Similarly, to test your **writing** ability, you will be given up to three sentences in English, and you must successfully write out at least one of the three sentences in order to pass.
- The content of the reading and writing sentences will focus on US history and civics topics.

The civics test will require you to show that you are familiar with the history and the system of government of the United States.

- All civics questions are taken from a pool of 100 questions.
- If you are at least 65 years old and have been a US permanent resident for at least 20 years, the question pool for your interview is only 20 questions (those marked with an asterisk '*').
- You will be asked up to 10 questions.
- You must answer at least 6 questions correctly in order to pass.

If you fail to pass one or both sections of the test, you will have another chance to pass the section or sections you failed in a second interview that will take place 60-90 days later.

Some of the content that appears in this guide is taken or adapted from USCIS Form M-638.

2

English Test

Reading Test

During your interview, you will be asked to read three sentences so the interviewer can verify that you are able to read English acceptably well. The only words that may be included on these sentences are those in the list below. As you may gather from this list, the sentences will focus on civics and history topics.

People

Abraham Lincoln
George Washington

Civics

American flag
Bill of Rights
capital
citizen
city
Congress
country
Father of Our Country
government
President
right
Senators
state/states
White House

Places

America
United States

U.S. Holidays

Presidents' Day
Memorial Day
Flag Day
Independence Day
Labor Day
Columbus Day
Thanksgiving

Question Words

How
What
When
Where
Who
Why

Verbs

can
come
do/does
elects
have/has
is/are/was/be
lives/lived
meet
name
pay
vote
want

Other (Function)

a
for
here
in
of
on
the
to
we

Other (Content)

colors
dollar bill
first
largest
many
most
north
one
people
second
south

3

Practice Reading Sentences

Below are some examples of the types of sentences you may be asked to read.

1. A citizen can vote for the President.

2. George Washington was the first President of the United States.

3. We can come here for Independence Day.

4. George Washington is on the one dollar bill.

5. The President lives in the United States capital city.

6. Who elects Senators to Congress?

7. What are the colors of the American flag?

8. We have the right to vote for what we want.

9. Abraham Lincoln lived in the White House.

10. When does Congress meet to vote?

11. We the people have the Bill of Rights.

12. George Washington was the Father of Our Country.

13. The government is of the people and for the people.

14. We come to the city to vote.

15. We meet many people in America.

16. What is the name of the United States President?

17. The state Senators vote for the country.

18. We want to come to the White House for President's Day.

19. The United States is in North America.

20. When can we meet the President?

21. Who are the state Senators?

22. What is the capital city of the United States?

23. Many people lived in the largest city in the country.

24. Where do the people of Congress meet?

25. Most people in the states want to vote.

Writing Test

During your interview, you will also be asked to write three sentences so the interviewer can verify that you are able to write in English acceptably well. Once again, all of the words you may be asked to write are included on the list below. Note that this list is slightly different from the list of words for the reading test.

People

Adams
Lincoln
Washington

Civics

American Indians
capital
citizens
Civil War
Congress
Father of Our Country
flag
free
freedom of speech
President
right
Senators
state/states
White House

Places

Alaska
California
Delaware
Mexico
New York City
United States
Washington
Washington, D.C.

Months

February
May
June
July
September
October
November

Holidays

Presidents' Day
Memorial Day
Flag Day
Independence Day
Labor Day
Columbus Day
Thanksgiving

Verbs

can
come
elect
have/has
is/was/be
lives/lived
meets
pay
vote
want

Other (Function)

and
during
for
here
in
of
on
the
to
we

Other (Content)

blue
dollar bill
fifty/50
first
largest
most
north
one
one hundred/100
people
red
second
south
taxes
white

Practice Writing Sentences

Below are some examples of the types of sentences you may be asked to write. Remember that the interviewer will be reading these sentences to you. You will not get to see them written down, so to best simulate the interview, you should have someone else read these sentences to you so you can practice writing them.

1. President's Day is in February.

2. The White House is in Washington, D.C.

3. The people vote to elect the President.

4. Washington was the Father of our Country.

5. Mexico is south of the United States.

6. Delaware was the first state.

7. Freedom of speech is the right of United States citizens.

8. The President lives in the White House.

9. The United States flag is red, white, and blue.

10. Alaska is the largest state.

11. We elect Senators to Congress.

12. Washington, D.C. is the capital of the United States.

13. The United States has fifty states.

14. Labor Day is in September.

15. United States citizens have the right to vote.

16. The state of California has the most people.

17. Citizens elect the President in November.

18. Congress meets to vote on taxes.

19. Washington is on the one dollar bill.

20. Lincoln lived during the Civil War.

21. Independence Day is in July.

22. Adams was the second President of the United States.

23. Columbus Day is in October.

Civics Questions and Answers

American Government

A. PRINCIPLES OF AMERICAN DEMOCRACY

1. What is the supreme law of the land?

- the Constitution

The Constitution was established in 1789 as the "supreme law of the land" and has lasted longer than any other country's constitution. It establishes the basic principles of the United States government and lists fundamental rights for all citizens and other people living in the United States.

2. What does the Constitution do?

- sets up the government
- defines the government
- protects basic rights of Americans

The Constitution establishes the structure of the government at the federal and state level and further defines the role of the three branches each of these levels are broken into. It also outlines the individual rights and liberties of each American citizen.

3. The idea of self-government is in the first three words of the Constitution. What are these words?

- We the People

The first words of the Constitution are "We the People" to emphasize that Americans would govern Americans and not foreign powers or monarchs. Normal citizens would create the government, work in the government, and prosper from the government.

4. What is an amendment?

- a change (to the Constitution)
- an addition (to the Constitution)

An amendment changes or adds to the Constitution. An amendment may alter a portion that already exists, such as rewording an existing law, or it may add something entirely new. There are a total of 27 amendments to the US Constitution.

9

5. What do we call the first ten amendments to the Constitution?

- the Bill of Rights

The original writers of the Constitution would not agree to sign it unless amendments were included that guaranteed and protected the rights of American citizens and limited the power of the government. These first 10 amendments of the Constitution are called the Bill of Rights.

6. What is one right or freedom from the First Amendment?

- speech
- religion
- assembly
- press
- petition the government

The First Amendment outlines the five ways a person's right to freedom of expression is protected from being prohibited or restricted by the government. An American citizen may speak freely, practice their religion freely, protest in a peaceful manner freely, spread public news freely, and petition the government for change freely.

7. How many amendments does the Constitution have?

- twenty-seven (27)

A total of 27 amendments to the Constitution have been ratified since its conception. The first 10 comprise the Bill of Rights and the 27th amendment was ratified in 1992.

8. What did the Declaration of Independence do?

- announced our independence (from Great Britain)
- declared our independence (from Great Britain)
- said that the United States is free (from Great Britain)

As the name suggests, the Declaration of Independence was a written declaration stating that the American colonies no longer consented to British control and are, and should be, free and independent states. The Declaration of Independence was approved by the Second Continental Congress on July 4th, 1776.

9. What are two rights in the Declaration of Independence?

- life
- liberty
- pursuit of happiness

The Declaration of Independence described what the Founding Fathers believed to be the natural or "unalienable" rights of all men. "We hold these truths to be self-evident, that all men are created equal, that they are endowed by their Creator with certain unalienable Rights, that among these are Life, Liberty and the pursuit of Happiness."

10. What is freedom of religion?

- You can practice any religion, or not practice a religion.

The freedom of religion is a guaranteed right contained within the First Amendment. It states that Congress cannot make laws that would establish a national religion or restrict a citizen's right to practice their religion or lack thereof.

11. What is the economic system in the United States?*

- capitalist economy
- market economy

The United States operates under a capitalist economy. Also called a market economy, capitalism means that most businesses are privately owned and operated for profit, rather than regulated or controlled by the government. Citizens are allowed to engage in the free and open trade of goods and services with minimal governmental restriction or influence.

12. What is the "rule of law"?

- Everyone must follow the law.
- Leaders must obey the law.
- Government must obey the law.
- No one is above the law.

The established "rule of law" means that no person or group is exempt from the law. Every American citizen is held accountable to the law, even the president.

B: SYSTEM OF GOVERNMENT

13. Name one branch or part of the government.*

- Congress
- legislative
- President
- executive
- the courts
- judicial

The first three articles of the Constitution define and outline the three branches of government. The Legislative branch, or Congress, creates new laws. The Executive branch, run by the President, carries out and enforces these laws. And the Judicial branch, also known as the courts, determines whether these laws follow the constitution.

14. What stops one branch of government from becoming too powerful?

- checks and balances
- separation of powers

Rather than have one person or group have the sole authority to create, enforce, and interpret law, the Constitution separates these powers between the three branches of government. Each branch is able to check or stop specific actions from the other two branches in a system of checks and balances that limits the power any individual branch can exert over American citizens.

15. Who is in charge of the executive branch?

- the President

The executive branch, run by the President, accepts or vetoes bills that have been passed by Congress. If the President accepts the bill, it becomes a law to then be interpreted by the Supreme Court. However, if the President vetoes or rejects the bill, it returns to Congress to be voted on again. The executive branch also enforces the laws of the United States.

16. Who makes federal laws?

- Congress
- Senate and House (of Representatives)
- (U.S. or national) legislature

Federal laws are created by Congress, but they are not enforced unless the President accepts them. If the President vetoes a bill, the bill is returned to Congress to be voted on again. If the bill passes with a two-thirds majority in both the House and the Senate, the veto can be overturned to become a law to be interpreted by the Supreme Court.

17. What are the two parts of the U.S. Congress?*

- the Senate and House (of Representatives)

Congress consists of two distinct chambers or houses called the House of Representatives and the Senate. Both chambers are filled with elected officials from all fifty states who work together to create laws and fulfill other legislative duties.

18. How many U.S. Senators are there?

- one hundred (100)

The Senate is composed of 100 total members, consisting of two elected officials from each state. Each state is represented by two senators regardless of the population size of their respective state. This was deliberately intended in order to give equal representation amongst all states, as opposed to the House of Representatives which bases representation in proportion to population size. Senators draft and vote on federal legislation and serve as the court for impeachment cases.

19. We elect a U.S. Senator for how many years?

- six (6)

Each senator is elected for a 6-year term, but there is no limit to how many total years a senator may serve if they are continually re-elected. These longer terms help offset the shorter 2-year terms of representatives of the House and encourage senators to be more focused on long-term prosperity rather than short-term public opinion.

20. Who is one of your state's U.S. Senators now?*

- Answers will vary depending on your location. Visit mometrix.com/uscitizen or scan the QR code below to find the most up to date correct answer for your test.

Alex Padilla
Laphonza Butler

21. The House of Representatives has how many voting members?

- four hundred thirty-five (435)

The House of Representatives has 435 total voting members with at least one representative from each state. The Constitution requires a census to be taken every ten years to redetermine how many representatives each state will be allowed. Representatives draft and vote on legislation and have the ability to begin impeachment proceedings. However, these proceedings are tried in the Senate.

22. We elect a U.S. Representative for how many years?

- two (2)

A representative is elected for a 2-year term, but there is no limit to how many total years a representative may serve if they are continually re-elected. The short-term nature of the position helps ensure that representatives are highly concerned with the desires and opinions of their constituents without being so short that no meaningful work gets accomplished.

23. Name your U.S. Representative.

- Answers will vary depending on your location. Visit mometrix.com/uscitizen or scan the QR code below to find the most up to date correct answer for your test.

Sara Jacobs

24. Who does a U.S. Senator represent?

- all people of the state

Senators represent the people of the state they were elected in.

25. Why do some states have more Representatives than other states?

- (because of) the state's population
- (because) they have more people
- (because) some states have more people

States with the largest portions of the population are allowed more representatives in the House to better reflect the interests of those states; however, each state must have at least one representative regardless of how many people live there. The Senate balances this by requiring exactly two senators per state, so less populated states have equal representation.

26. We elect a President for how many years?

- four (4)

A president's term lasts for 4 years and may only serve a total of 2 terms. This means a person can only be President for 8 years collectively.

27. In what month do we vote for President?*

- November

The Presidential election occurs in November, and the winner is sworn into office in January of the following year.

28. What is the name of the President of the United States now?*

- Joseph R. Biden, Jr.
- Joe Biden
- Biden

Once a former Vice President, Joe Biden was elected as the 46th President of the United States in November of 2020.

29. What is the name of the Vice President of the United States now?

- Kamala D. Harris
- Kamala Harris
- Harris

Joe Biden selected Kamala Harris as his Vice President, making her the 49th Vice President of the United States.

30. If the President can no longer serve, who becomes President?

- the Vice President

If the President dies, resigns, or becomes otherwise unfit or unable to fulfill the duties of the position, the Vice President will be sworn in as the President.

31. If both the President and the Vice President can no longer serve, who becomes President?

- the Speaker of the House

If both the President and Vice President die, resign, or become otherwise unable to fulfill the duties of their positions, the succession falls to the speaker of the House of Representatives.

32. Who is the Commander in Chief of the military?

- the President

The President is the ultimate military authority of the United States also known as the Commander in Chief. Although the President commands the military, only Congress can declare war.

33. Who signs bills to become laws?

- the President

The President has the authority to sign bills drafted by Congress to turn them into laws. If after 10 days the President has chosen not to sign the bill and Congress is still in session, the bill will automatically become a law.

34. Who vetoes bills?

- the President

The President also has the authority to veto bills. If the President vetoes a bill, it returns to Congress again to be voted on by both Houses. If the bill passes with a two-thirds majority in both Houses, the veto is overturned and the bill becomes a law. If after 10 days the President has chosen not to sign the bill and Congress has adjourned, the bill is automatically rejected and does not become a law.

35. What does the President's Cabinet do?

- advises the President

The President's Cabinet consists of the advisory staff that the President places in charge of the various executive departments. These staff members are usually referred to as the secretaries of their particular department, and they keep the President apprised of their department's affairs and offer counsel when required.

36. What are two Cabinet-level positions?

Attorney General	Secretary of Homeland Security
Vice President	Secretary of Housing and Urban Development
Secretary of Agriculture	Secretary of the Interior
Secretary of Commerce	Secretary of Labor
Secretary of Defense	Secretary of State
Secretary of Education	Secretary of Transportation
Secretary of Energy	Secretary of the Treasury
Secretary of Health and Human Services	Secretary of Veterans Affairs

Including the Vice President, the President's Cabinet contains 16 total members.

37. What does the judicial branch do?

- reviews laws
- explains laws
- resolves disputes (disagreements)
- decides if a law goes against the Constitution

The judicial branch reviews and interprets laws by comparing them to the Constitution. It is composed of a hierarchical system of courts with the Supreme Court at the top. Even if a bill is passed by Congress and signed by the President to become a law, the Supreme Court can judge that law to be unconstitutional and render it invalid.

38. What is the highest court in the United States?

- the Supreme Court

The federal court system is separated into three tiers. The first and lowest tier includes ninety-four district or trial courts. The second and intermediate tier includes thirteen appellate courts that are organized into twelve regional circuits. The third and highest tier is the Supreme Court.

39. How many justices are on the Supreme Court?

- nine (9)

There are currently nine Supreme Court justices, one chief and eight associates, but there is no law that mandates this specific number. Supreme Court justices are nominated by the President and serve a lifelong term. For more information on the Supreme Court, go to www.supremecourt.gov.

40. Who is the Chief Justice of the United States now?

- John Roberts (John G. Roberts, Jr.)

The 17th and current Chief Justice of the United States is John G. Roberts, Jr. He became chief justice at the age of 50 after the death of former chief justice William Rehnquist. The Chief Justice's vote is equivalent to the other associate justices.

41. Under our Constitution, some powers belong to the federal government. What is one power of the federal government?

- to print money
- to declare war
- to create an army
- to make treaties

The federal government is given specific and limited powers by the Constitution. Some of these delegated powers include the ability to print currency, to declare war, to create an army, and to make treaties with foreign nations as needed. Powers not explicitly rendered to the federal government belong to the states or the people.

42. Under our Constitution, some powers belong to the states. What is one power of the states?

- provide schooling and education
- provide protection (police)
- provide safety (fire departments)
- give a driver's license
- approve zoning and land use

Powers not explicitly rendered unto the federal government are considered reserved to the state government or the people directly. Some of these reserved state powers include the provision of schooling and education, public safety in the form of police and fire departments, and the issuance of driver's licenses.

43. Who is the Governor of your state now?

- Answers will vary depending on your location. Visit <u>mometrix.com/uscitizen</u> or scan the QR code below to find the most up to date correct answer for your test.

Gavin Newsom

State governments have the same branch structure as the national government. The chief executive office of the state is the Governor, and they enforce and execute the laws of their state as the President does for the national government. The powers of the Governor are outlined by the state or territory's constitution in which they serve.

Residents of the District of Columbia should answer that it does not have a Governor.

44. What is the capital of your state?*

- Answers will vary depending on your location. Visit <u>mometrix.com/uscitizen</u> or scan the QR code below to find the most up to date correct answer for your test.

Sacramento

Similar to the nation's capital, each state has its own capital as well. These capital cities will contain major offices of the state legislative branch.

45. What are the two major political parties in the United States?*

- Democratic and Republican

The two major political parties of the United States are the Democratic and Republican parties.

46. What is the political party of the President now?

- Democratic (Party)

President Joseph Biden is a member of the Democratic party.

47. What is the name of the Speaker of the House of Representatives now?

- Nancy Pelosi
- Pelosi

Note: This answer is correct **through January 3, 2023** when the 118th Congress is sworn in and a speaker is elected for the term. Visit mometrix.com/uscitizen or scan the QR code below to find the most up to date correct answer for your test.

mike Johnson †

SCAN HERE

C: Rights and Responsibilities

48. There are four amendments to the Constitution about who can vote. Describe one of them.

- Citizens eighteen (18) and older (can vote).
- You don't have to pay (a poll tax) to vote.
- Any citizen can vote. (Women and men can vote.)
- A male citizen of any race (can vote).

Since its inception, the Constitution has been amended four times concerning voting regulations. In 1776, only white, land-owning men aged 21 or older had the right to vote. Over time, this right has expanded to all American citizens of any race or gender aged 18 or older. Additionally, voting no longer requires the ownership of land or the payment of a poll tax.

49. What is one responsibility that is only for United States citizens?*

- serve on a jury
- vote in a federal election

Sometimes referred to as civic duties, each American citizen is given two civil responsibilities. Each American citizen has the responsibility to serve on a jury when selected unless they have a qualifying exemption. Secondly, citizens have the right and responsibility to vote in a federal election to determine who will become the President.

50. Name one right only for United States citizens.

- vote in a federal election
- run for federal office

United States citizens are granted rights and privileges that are not necessarily guaranteed to citizens of other nations. American citizens have the right and responsibility to vote in a federal election to determine who will become the President, and they have the right to run for federal office if they meet the other mandated requirements for the position.

51. What are two rights of everyone living in the United States?

- freedom of expression
- freedom of speech
- freedom of assembly
- freedom to petition the government
- freedom of religion
- the right to bear arms

Some rights in the Constitution are granted to all people living in America, not just citizens. The freedoms outlined in the First Amendment and the right to bear arms are granted to all citizens and non-citizens alike when living in this country, though there are some requirements for procuring firearms.

52. What do we show loyalty to when we say the Pledge of Allegiance?

- the United States
- the flag

The Pledge of Allegiance begins with the phrase, "I pledge allegiance to the Flag of the United States of America" to illustrate the important symbolism of the flag to our nation. It serves as the banner for the belief that America should always be a free and unified nation where there is liberty and justice for all.

53. What is one promise you make when you become a United States citizen?

- give up loyalty to other countries
- defend the Constitution and laws of the United States
- obey the laws of the United States
- serve in the U.S. military (if needed)
- serve (do important work for) the nation (if needed)
- be loyal to the United States

The final step to becoming an American citizen is to swear the Oath of Allegiance at a naturalization ceremony. The oath includes giving up loyalty to other countries and being loyal to the United States, defending the Constitution and obeying the laws of the United States, and serving in the U.S. military or doing important work for the nation if needed.

54. How old do citizens have to be to vote for President?*

- eighteen (18) and older

The minimum voting age for federal, state, and local elections is 18 years old for all American citizens with few restrictions (some areas allow citizens aged 16 or above to vote in local elections only). Depending on the state of residence, there are voting restrictions imposed on citizens who have been convicted of certain crimes or are mentally incapacitated. Citizens who live in U.S. territories are unable to vote for the President in the general election.

55. What are two ways that Americans can participate in their democracy?

vote	call Senators and Representatives
join a political party	publicly support or oppose an issue or policy
help with a campaign	run for office
join a civic group	write to a newspaper
join a community group	call Senators and Representatives
give an elected official your opinion on an issue	

America was founded on the idea that the government should always function to benefit and serve the people under its authority. However, this requires that citizens participate in governmental processes to ensure that their beliefs and needs are being upheld. Every citizen is encouraged to actively participate in the democratic process so that no opinion goes unheard.

56. When is the last day you can send in federal income tax forms?*

- April 15

Federal income tax forms must be filed by the fifteenth day of April every year. If there are ever sufficiently extenuating circumstances that would extend this deadline, the government will deliver written notification of this extension and the newly designated deadline for filing.

57. When must all men register for the Selective Service?

- at age eighteen (18)
- between eighteen (18) and twenty-six (26)

All male citizens between the ages of 18 and 26 are required to register for Selective Service, commonly referred to as the military draft. Registration is required within 30 days of turning 18, but late registrations are accepted until turning 26. Failure to register is considered a federal offense punishable by up to five years in prison and/or a fine of up to $250,000. Registration is available at a United States post office or on the internet at www.sss.gov.

American History

A: COLONIAL PERIOD AND INDEPENDENCE

58. What is one reason colonists came to America?

- freedom
- political liberty
- religious freedom
- economic opportunity
- practice their religion
- escape persecution

In the early 1600s, colonists from all over England and Europe began making their way to the American colonies with the hope of building a better life. Many colonists fled their countries to avoid religious or political persecution, while others sought a new life of economic opportunity. America continues to be a land of freedom and opportunity for people around the world who want to try and build a better life.

59. Who lived in America before the Europeans arrived?

- American Indians
- Native Americans

Generations of American Indians lived in America before the first European Pilgrims ever arrived in the colonies in the early 1600s. Some Native Americans, specifically the Wampanoag tribe, shared their experience and teaching with the new colonists to help them grow crops for food. As more settlers began moving to America, the lack of available space caused them to migrate further inland onto the territory of Native American tribes. This led to confrontation, and ultimately violence, as these colonists used their superior technology and weaponry to conquer the Native Americans and take their land for themselves.

60. What group of people was taken to America and sold as slaves?

- Africans
- people from Africa

Although slavery existed in many countries long before America was founded, by the year 1700, the colonists had begun importing slaves from Africa to use as a labor force. Men, women, and children were bought and sold like cattle and worked without payment or basic rights. Slavery remained legal in America until the 13th Amendment was ratified in 1865 after the end of the Civil War.

61. Why did the colonists fight the British?

- because of high taxes (taxation without representation)
- because the British army stayed in their houses (boarding, quartering)
- because they didn't have self-government

The Declaration of Independence and resultant Revolutionary War were the culmination of years of bitterness and anger the colonists had against the British. The colonists were given no representation in government and yet taxed against their wishes. They were also forced to let British soldiers stay in their homes and were not even allowed to elect their own representatives. Eventually, these grievances grew to be unbearable, and the colonists revolted against British rule.

62. Who wrote the Declaration of Independence?

- (Thomas) Jefferson

Thomas Jefferson wrote the Declaration of Independence in 1776 in roughly seventeen days to formally outline the reasons why the colonists believed they should be a free and independent nation because they no longer consented to British governance.

63. When was the Declaration of Independence adopted?

- July 4, 1776

The Declaration of Independence was adopted by the Second Continental Congress on July 4, 1776, but the United States would not ultimately win its freedom from Great Britain until the end of the Revolutionary War in 1783.

64. There were 13 original states. Name three.

New Hampshire	North Carolina
Delaware	New York
Massachusetts	South Carolina
Maryland	New Jersey
Rhode Island	Georgia
Virginia	Pennsylvania
Connecticut	

After winning the Revolutionary War, the newly independent states began the process of determining how they would govern themselves. An initial attempt known as the Articles of Confederation was insufficient for maintaining unity, so a new document needed to be written. This document, known as the Constitution, was agreed upon and ratified over time by the former colonies until there were 13 formally united states.

65. What happened at the Constitutional Convention?

- The Constitution was written.
- The Founding Fathers wrote the Constitution.

The Articles of Confederation created a national government that was too weak to unite the newly independent states, and almost led to the destabilization of the states as a whole. As a result, delegates from all but one of the states met in 1787 at the Constitutional Convention with the initial intent of creating amendments for the Articles of Confederation. However, they soon realized that a new document would be necessary before the states would agree. On September 17, 1787, 39 of 55 total delegates signed the new Constitution before introducing it to the states for ratification.

66. When was the Constitution written?

- 1787

The Constitution was written in 1787, but it was not ratified by all 13 states for another three years. Rhode Island ratified the Constitution in 1790, making it the last of the original 13 states to do so.

67. The Federalist Papers supported the passage of the U.S. Constitution. Name one of the writers.

- (James) Madison
- (Alexander) Hamilton
- (John) Jay
- Publius

Even after the Constitution was written, many states were still not satisfied with it. In an attempt to sway the people to ratify it as national law, some of the Constitution's writers began writing a series of persuasive essays for New York newspapers under the pen name "Publius." The goal of these papers was to better explain sections of the Constitution and describe why the states would benefit from its ratification. These 85 papers were eventually combined and published together in a book called *The Federalist*.

68. What is one thing Benjamin Franklin is famous for?

- U.S. diplomat
- oldest member of the Constitutional Convention
- first Postmaster General of the United States
- writer of "Poor Richard's Almanac"
- started the first free libraries

Benjamin Franklin was a brilliant inventor, an astute diplomat, and the oldest member of the Constitutional Convention. He wrote an autobiography and the very popular *Poor Richard's Almanac* and was named the first Postmaster General of the United States. His face is displayed on the $100 bill.

69. Who is the "Father of Our Country"?

- (George) Washington

George Washington was the first American president and the leader of the Continental Army that won the Revolutionary War against Great Britain. His leadership helped unite the country and is one of the greatest figures in American history. By the time he was unanimously elected as President in 1789, many people and publications around the nation had already begun describing him as the "Father of Our Country." This title endured and remains to this day, although its first usage is unclear.

70. Who was the first President?*

- (George) Washington

George Washington was unanimously elected as the first President of the United States despite him not wanting the position initially. He was sworn in on April 30th, 1789 and delivered a speech that would be known as the first Presidential Inaugural Address. Although the Constitution only requires that the President be sworn in and recite the oath of office, every President since Washington has given their own address as well.

B: 1800s

71. What territory did the United States buy from France in 1803?

- the Louisiana Territory
- Louisiana

In 1803, President Thomas Jefferson bought the Louisiana Territory from France for $15 million, or approximately 3 cents an acre. This ultimately doubled the size of the U.S. and gave it unhindered access to the great port city of New Orleans and the shipping channels of the Mississippi River.

72. Name one war fought by the United States in the 1800s.

- War of 1812
- Mexican-American War
- Civil War
- Spanish-American War

Continued resentment from the revolutionary War and escalating tensions between Great Britain and the United States finally reached a breaking point in 1812. The British had begun seizing American ships to prevent trade with France and forcing American seamen to serve on British ships. This was combined with the fact that the British were also supplying guns to the Native Americans which made American attempts to expand into the Northwest Territory significantly more dangerous. The war lasted three years, with an overall victory for America, but the U.S. Capitol was burned down by the British in the fighting.

As the United States continued to expand and settle more territory, it eventually decided to annex the Republic of Texas in 1845. Texas had fought for its independence from Mexico a decade earlier, but Mexico did not accept the Rio Grande as the border between Texas and Mexico. This tension eventually led to armed conflict, with the United States declaring war in 1846. The United States defeated Mexico on the battlefield after overtaking the capital, Mexico City, in 1847. The Treaty of Guadalupe was eventually agreed to by both nations which ended the war officially in 1848, as well as earned a significant amount of territory for the United States.

Tensions over states' rights, the economy, and slavery ultimately led to the Civil War between the northern and southern halves of the United States. The pro-slavery South seceded to form the Confederacy, while the anti-slavery Union of the North fought to keep the states united. The war lasted from 1861 to 1865, when the Confederate army, led by Robert E. Lee, surrendered to Ulysses S. Grant. The Civil War still remains, to this day, the deadliest military conflict in American history, with more American lives lost than any other war.

When America began pursuing economic interests in Cuba, Cuba was currently seeking independence from Spain. The United States supported Cuba in its efforts for independence, but this caused tension between Spain and the United States. The mysterious explosion of the U.S.S. Maine in Cuba caused a tipping point, and the United States declared war on Spain in 1898. Conflict only lasted three months before the United States obtained a decisive victory and ended the war with the Treaty of Paris of 1898. This earned the United States Guam, Puerto Rico, and the Philippines.

73. Name the U.S. war between the North and the South.

- the Civil War
- the War between the States

Also known as the War between the States, the Civil War was fought by the northern states, or the Union, and the southern states, or the Confederacy. The North defeated the South after four years of war, in 1865. As a result, the southern states were readopted into the Union after their secession, and slavery became illegal throughout the United States.

74. Name one problem that led to the Civil War.

- slavery
- economic reasons
- states' rights

Tensions over states' rights, the economy, and slavery ultimately led to the Civil War between the northern and southern halves of the United States. The South's reliance on slave labor for nearly all of its economy, and the anti-slavery position of the North, made a war over the legality of slavery and the nature of states' rights nearly inevitable. The South seceded into the Confederate States of America and fought against the collective northern states called the Union. The Union army defeated the Confederate army in 1865.

75. What was one important thing that Abraham Lincoln did?*

- freed the slaves (Emancipation Proclamation)
- saved (or preserved) the Union
- led the United States during the Civil War

Abraham Lincoln was sworn in as the 16th President of the United States in 1861. The election of an anti-slavery President prompted the South to begin their plan of succession. Lincoln led the United States during the Civil War and made sure that the South would rejoin the Union as a condition of surrender to make the states united again. His appointed generals led the Union army to victory and his Emancipation Proclamation freed the slaves throughout the Confederacy.

76. What did the Emancipation Proclamation do?

- freed the slaves
- freed slaves in the Confederacy
- freed slaves in the Confederate states
- freed slaves in most Southern states

Two years into the Civil War, President Lincoln issued the Emancipation Proclamation on January 1st, 1863. It stated that slaves living in the southern or Confederate states were now free. As a result, many slaves joined and fought for the Union army. Unfortunately, the Emancipation proclamation did not include slaves in states not actively rebelling against the North, and it was not until the 13th amendment was passed after the end of the Civil War that slavery was made illegal throughout the United States.

77. What did Susan B. Anthony do?

- fought for women's rights
- fought for civil rights

Susan B. Anthony is most well known for her abolition efforts to free slaves and fighting for women to be able to vote. Her work was instrumental in uniting women to her cause and the eventual passing of the 19th amendment in 1920. She dedicated her life to the belief that men and women of every color should have equal rights.

C: Recent American History and Other Important Historical Information

78. Name one war fought by the United States in the 1900s.*

- World War I
- World War II
- Korean War
- Vietnam War
- (Persian) Gulf War

World War I began in 1914 after the assassination of Archduke Ferdinand and quickly turned into a global conflict separated into two sides known as the Central Powers and the Allies. However, the United States refused to enter the war until 1917 when German submarines began using unrestricted submarine warfare to sink U.S. ships that were neutral in the war. This made ships hesitant to sail, which caused food shortages and hurt trade. Although the Treaty of Versailles officially ended the war in 1919, the U.S. did not ratify the treaty and instead formally ended its involvement after the Knox-Porter Resolution in 1921. The harsh sanctions placed against Germany in the treaty of Versailles laid the groundwork for German resentment and the eventual beginnings of World War II.

World War II is generally considered to have begun after the joint invasion of Poland by Nazi Germany and the Soviet Union in 1939. Soon after, the conflict began to spread across the globe as Germany invaded more territory and countries began forming alliances and picking sides. The Axis powers consisted of Germany, Italy, and Japan, and the Allies consisted of France, Great Britain, and ultimately the Soviet Union after Germany broke the Molotov-Ribbentrop Pact. The United States refrained from entering the war until the Japanese attack on Pearl Harbor in 1941 caused them to join the Allies. The war continued until the eventual defeat of Nazi Germany and the surrender of Japan in 1945.

After the surrender of Japan in 1945, Korea was split into two occupation zones divided at the 38th parallel. The northern occupation zone remained under communist influence, whereas the southern zone sought to establish a democratic government with support from the United States and its allies. In 1950, forces from North Korea began an invasion into the South Korea which led to retaliation by the United Nations. The United States provided the bulk of the military support and pushed back the invading forces. Conflict continued until 1953, when the Korean Armistice Agreement was signed and ended the Korean War.

The Vietnam War was the second of the Indochina Wars between communist supported North Vietnam and anti-communist supported South Vietnam. After French forces formally pulled out of Vietnam territory in 1954, the United States became heavily invested in winning the war for South Vietnam. After years of conflict, Congress gave President Lyndon B. Johnson approval in 1964 to massively increase U.S. combat presence in Vietnam, hoping to bring the war to a close and secure a decisive victory. Despite the increased force, the United States did not manage to secure the victory they desired; and as the anti-war sentiment began to grow in the United States, President Richard M. Nixon made the decision to gradually withdraw American troops from 1969 to 1973. The North Vietnamese forces captured the South Vietnam capital of Saigon in 1975, bringing the war to a close. Vietnam became a single, communist nation one year later in 1976.

The Persian Gulf War began as a response to the Iraqi invasion of Kuwait in 1990. Iraq's actions were met with fairly unanimous condemnation from the United Nations, and the United States and Great Britain deployed troops into Saudi Arabia while calling other nations to do the same. Many countries agreed to join the American-led coalition, and within a month, the coalition had driven back Iraqi forces out of Kuwait. The coalition declared a ceasefire after the successful liberation of Kuwait in 1991.

79. Who was President during World War I?

- (Woodrow) Wilson

Woodrow Wilson served as the President of the United States during World War I. Initially hesitant to get the United States involved, Wilson eventually called for Congress to declare war after Germany violated its oath to cease unrestricted submarine warfare and tried to bribe Mexico into an alliance against the United States.

80. Who was President during the Great Depression and World War II?

- (Franklin) Roosevelt

Franklin Delano Roosevelt (FDR) was president of the United States during both the Great Depression and World War II. He is the only President to serve four terms in office, from 1933 until 1945. His "New Deal" program established the Social Security Administration that still exists today, and commanded the United States armed forces throughout most of World War II before his early passing in 1945.

81. Who did the United States fight in World War II?

- Japan, Germany, and Italy

World War II was fought by the Axis powers and the Allied forces. The Axis powers consisted of Japan, Germany, and Italy. The Allies consisted of the United States, France, Great Britain, and the Soviet Union. It was the deadliest military conflict in the history of the world, with death estimates ranging from 50 million to 80 million people worldwide, of which a major percentage were civilians.

82. Before he was President, Eisenhower was a general. What war was he in?

- World War II

President Dwight D. Eisenhower served as a five-star General of the Army and Supreme Commander of the Allied Expeditionary Force during World War II. He supervised the planning and successful invasion of Normandy, France in 1944, commonly known as D-Day.

31

83. During the Cold War, what was the main concern of the United States?

- Communism

After World War II, the United States and its allies were afraid that the Soviet Union would spread its communistic ideals across the globe. This fear led to a decades-long period of political and military unrest between the United States and the Soviet Union known as the Cold War. The Cold War lasted over 40 years until the dissolution of the Soviet Union in 1991.

84. What movement tried to end racial discrimination?

- civil rights (movement)

The civil rights movement (1954-1968) attempted to end racial discrimination in the United States. Despite slavery being outlawed nearly a century prior, there remained many racially disparate policies and practices throughout America at the time. The civil rights movement made significant progress in ensuring equal rights for all citizens.

85. What did Martin Luther King, Jr. do?*

- fought for civil rights
- worked for equality for all Americans

Martin Luther King, Jr. was the main leader of the civil rights movement of the 1950s and 1960s. A powerful orator and leader, King inspired Americans to challenge the racially unjust laws of the day through nonviolent protests and petitions. His efforts to gain equality for all Americans earned him the Nobel Peace Prize in 1964, at the age of 35. King's "I Have a Dream" speech remains one of the most popular speeches to this day, and his legacy continues to inspire social reform decades later. Martin Luther King, Jr. was assassinated on April 4, 1968.

86. What major event happened on September 11, 2001, in the United States?

- Terrorists attacked the United States.

On September 11, 2001, members of the Al-Qaeda terrorist organization hijacked four airplanes flying out of U.S. airports to deliberately crash them into highly populated buildings. Two of the planes were flown into the Twin Towers of the World Trade Center in New York City, which ultimately resulted in both buildings collapsing. The third plane was flown into the Pentagon in Arlington, Virginia; and the fourth plane, although originally aimed at Washington, D.C., crashed in a field in Pennsylvania after a valiant struggle from passengers onboard. This coordinated act of terror left thousands dead and was the deadliest attack on American soil in the history of the United States.

87. Name one American Indian tribe in the United States.

[USCIS Officers will be supplied with a list of federally recognized American Indian tribes.]

Cherokee	Oneida
Cheyenne	Apache
Navajo	Lakota
Arawak	Iroquois
Sioux	Crow
Shawnee	Creek
Chippewa	Teton
Mohegan	Blackfeet
Choctaw	Hopi
Huron	Seminole
Pueblo	Inuit

Because there are hundreds of federally recognized American Indian tribes in the United States, the USCIS Officers will have an updated and comprehensive list available to them.

Long before European settlers ever set foot on American soil, American Indians (or Native Americans) inhabited this land. American Indian tribes vary drastically in their cultural heritage and the traditions they celebrate. Although there are designated areas of land known as reservations given specifically to American Indian tribes, the vast majority of American Indians reside outside of them.

Integrated Civics

A: GEOGRAPHY

88. Name one of the two longest rivers in the United States.

- Missouri (River)
- Mississippi (River)

The two longest rivers in the United States are the Missouri River and the Mississippi River. The Missouri River is 2,341 miles long and is longer than the Mississippi River by one mile. The Missouri River begins in Three Forks, Montana and ends in St. Louis, Missouri before emptying into the Mississippi River. The Mississippi River begins in Lake Itasca, Minnesota and empties into the Gulf of Mexico

89. What ocean is on the West Coast of the United States?

- Pacific (Ocean)

The West Coast of the United States is bounded by the Pacific Ocean, while the East Coast is bounded by the Atlantic Ocean. The Pacific Ocean is the largest ocean in the world, and it borders a total of five states.

90. What ocean is on the East Coast of the United States?

- Atlantic (Ocean)

The East Coast of the United States is bounded by the Atlantic Ocean, while the West Coast is bounded by the Pacific Ocean. The Atlantic Ocean is the second largest ocean in the world, and it borders a total of fourteen states.

91. Name one U.S. territory.

- Puerto Rico
- U.S. Virgin Islands
- American Samoa
- Northern Mariana Islands
- Guam

There are five permanently inhabited U.S. territories and nine with no native population. Territories remain mostly self-governed, but they do fall under the authority of the United States. Residents born in Puerto Rico, the U.S. Virgin Islands, the Northern Mariana Islands, and Guam are all considered United States citizens, but those born is American Samoa are considered "non-citizen nationals." Each territory may send a delegate to the House of Representatives and vote in primary elections for president; however, they are not allowed to vote in the general elections for president.

92. Name one state that borders Canada.

Maine	Idaho
Minnesota	Pennsylvania
New Hampshire	Washington
North Dakota	Ohio
Vermont	Alaska
Montana	Michigan
New York	

Canada borders the United States to the north and shares more than 5,500 miles of border with thirteen states. The official boundary between the United States and Canada was established after the Revolutionary War and is currently overseen by the International Boundary Commission (*Commission de la frontière internationale*).

93. Name one state that borders Mexico.

- California
- Arizona
- New Mexico
- Texas

Mexico borders the United States to the south and shares more than 1,900 miles of border with four states The official boundary between the United States and Mexico was established after the end of the Mexican-American War and the Gadsden Purchase in 1853. It is currently overseen by the International Boundary and Water Commission (*Comisión Internacional de Límites y Aguas*).

94. What is the capital of the United States?*

- Washington, D.C.

The capital of the United States is located in Washington, D.C. It is home to the Capitol Building, the Supreme Court, and the White House, which allows for rapid communication and travel between all three branches of the federal government. In order to prevent any state from having specialized authority over the capital, the District of Columbia is under the exclusive jurisdiction of Congress and is neither a state, nor part of one.

95. Where is the Statue of Liberty?*

- New York (Harbor)
- Liberty Island

[Also acceptable are New Jersey, near New York City, and on the Hudson (River).]

France gave the Statue of Liberty to the United States as a gift in 1886. It is located on Liberty Island in New York Harbor, and it stands as a beacon of freedom and democracy to the American people and all who would seek to become citizens of the United States.

B: SYMBOLS

96. Why does the flag have 13 stripes?

- because there were 13 original colonies
- because the stripes represent the original colonies

The stripes on the United States flag represent the original 13 colonies that bravely fought for their independence in the Revolutionary War. As America expanded and more states began to join the country, Congress decided that the number of stripes should remain at 13, and instead let stars represent the number of states. This was intended to honor the bravery of the original colonies and still make a provision for future growth.

97. Why does the flag have 50 stars?*

- because there is one star for each state
- because each star represents a state
- because there are 50 states

The flag of the United States has 50 stars because each star represents a state. There are currently 50 total states after the addition of Hawaii in 1959.

98. What is the name of the national anthem?

- The Star-Spangled Banner

The national anthem is named the "Star-Spangled Banner." Its name originates from the first stanza of Francis Scott Key's poem, "Defence of Fort M'Henry," which describes his experience watching British forces attempt to conquer Fort McHenry. Despite hundreds of cannon shots being fired through the night, the dawn revealed the American flag still hung atop the fort, meaning the Americans had successfully repelled the British forces.

The Star-Spangled Banner
Oh, say, can you see, by the dawn's early light,
What so proudly we hailed at the twilight's last gleaming?
Whose broad stripes and bright stars, thro' the perilous fight;
O'er the ramparts we watched, were so gallantly streaming.
And the rockets' red glare, the bombs bursting in air,
Gave proof through the night that our flag was still there.
Oh, say, does that star-spangled banner yet wave
O'er the land of the free and the home of the brave?

C: Holidays

99. When do we celebrate Independence Day?*

- July 4

We celebrate Independence Day every year on July 4th to celebrate the adoption of the Declaration of Independence. It commemorates the bravery of the colonists who declared their freedom from Great Britain and is commonly called America's birthday.

100. Name two national U.S. holidays.

New Year's Day	Labor Day
Martin Luther King, Jr. Day	Columbus Day
Presidents' Day	Veterans Day
Memorial Day	Thanksgiving
Juneteenth	Christmas
Independence Day	

Congress has declared certain days to be federal holidays. Most federal employees will not be required to work on these days and most government offices will be closed. Juneteenth is the most recent addition to the national holiday list and is celebrated on June 19th.

Civics Question Pool

All of the questions that you may be asked on the civics section of the citizenship interview appear here without the answers. We recommend that you practice by having someone ask you questions from this list. This is the best way to simulate what you will experience at the interview. If you prefer to practice alone or quietly, you may write your answer in the space provided.

1. What is the supreme law of the land?

2. What does the Constitution do?

3. The idea of self-government is in the first three words of the Constitution. What are these words?

4. What is an amendment?

5. What do we call the first ten amendments to the Constitution?

6. What is one right or freedom from the First Amendment?

7. How many amendments does the Constitution have?

8. What did the Declaration of Independence do?

9. What are two rights in the Declaration of Independence?

10. What is freedom of religion?

11. What is the economic system in the United States?*

12. What is the "rule of law"?

13. Name one branch or part of the government.*

14. What stops one branch of government from becoming too powerful?

15. Who is in charge of the executive branch?

16. Who makes federal laws?

17. What are the two parts of the U.S. Congress?*

18. How many U.S. Senators are there?

19. We elect a U.S. Senator for how many years?

20. Who is one of your state's U.S. Senators now?*

21. The House of Representatives has how many voting members?

22. We elect a U.S. Representative for how many years?

23. Name your U.S. Representative.

24. Who does a U.S. Senator represent?

25. Why do some states have more Representatives than other states?

26. We elect a President for how many years?

27. In what month do we vote for President?*

28. What is the name of the President of the United States now?*

29. What is the name of the Vice President of the United States now?

30. If the President can no longer serve, who becomes President?

31. If both the President and the Vice President can no longer serve, who becomes President?

32. Who is the Commander in Chief of the military?

33. Who signs bills to become laws?

34. Who vetoes bills?

35. What does the President's Cabinet do?

36. What are two Cabinet-level positions?

37. What does the judicial branch do?

38. What is the highest court in the United States?

39. How many justices are on the Supreme Court?

40. Who is the Chief Justice of the United States now?

41. Under our Constitution, some powers belong to the federal government. What is one power of the federal government?

42. Under our Constitution, some powers belong to the states. What is one power of the states?

43. Who is the Governor of your state now?

44. What is the capital of your state?*

45. What are the two major political parties in the United States?*

46. What is the political party of the President now?

47. What is the name of the Speaker of the House of Representatives now?

48. There are four amendments to the Constitution about who can vote. Describe one of them.

49. What is one responsibility that is only for United States citizens?*

50. Name one right only for United States citizens.

51. What are two rights of everyone living in the United States?

52. What do we show loyalty to when we say the Pledge of Allegiance?

53. What is one promise you make when you become a United States citizen?

54. How old do citizens have to be to vote for President?*

55. What are two ways that Americans can participate in their democracy?

56. When is the last day you can send in federal income tax forms?*

57. When must all men register for the Selective Service?

58. What is one reason colonists came to America?

59. Who lived in America before the Europeans arrived?

60. What group of people was taken to America and sold as slaves?

61. Why did the colonists fight the British?

62. Who wrote the Declaration of Independence?

63. When was the Declaration of Independence adopted?

64. There were 13 original states. Name three.

65. What happened at the Constitutional Convention?

66. When was the Constitution written?

67. The Federalist Papers supported the passage of the U.S. Constitution. Name one of the writers.

68. What is one thing Benjamin Franklin is famous for?

69. Who is the "Father of Our Country"?

70. Who was the first President?*

71. What territory did the United States buy from France in 1803?

72. Name one war fought by the United States in the 1800s.

73. Name the U.S. war between the North and the South.

74. Name one problem that led to the Civil War.

75. What was one important thing that Abraham Lincoln did?*

76. What did the Emancipation Proclamation do?

77. What did Susan B. Anthony do?

78. Name one war fought by the United States in the 1900s.*

79. Who was President during World War I?

80. Who was President during the Great Depression and World War II?

81. Who did the United States fight in World War II?

82. Before he was President, Eisenhower was a general. What war was he in?

83. During the Cold War, what was the main concern of the United States?

84. What movement tried to end racial discrimination?

85. What did Martin Luther King, Jr. do?*

86. What major event happened on September 11, 2001, in the United States?

87. Name one American Indian tribe in the United States.

88. Name one of the two longest rivers in the United States.

89. What ocean is on the West Coast of the United States?

90. What ocean is on the East Coast of the United States?

91. Name one U.S. territory.

92. Name one state that borders Canada.

93. Name one state that borders Mexico.

94. What is the capital of the United States?*

95. Where is the Statue of Liberty?*

96. Why does the flag have 13 stripes?

97. Why does the flag have 50 stars?*

98. What is the name of the national anthem?

99. When do we celebrate Independence Day?*

100. Name two national U.S. holidays.

How to Overcome Test Anxiety

Just the thought of taking a test is enough to make most people a little nervous. A test is an important event that can have a long-term impact on your future, so it's important to take it seriously and it's natural to feel anxious about performing well. But just because anxiety is normal, that doesn't mean that it's helpful in test taking, or that you should simply accept it as part of your life. Anxiety can have a variety of effects. These effects can be mild, like making you feel slightly nervous, or severe, like blocking your ability to focus or remember even a simple detail.

If you experience test anxiety—whether severe or mild—it's important to know how to beat it. To discover this, first you need to understand what causes test anxiety.

Causes of Test Anxiety

While we often think of anxiety as an uncontrollable emotional state, it can actually be caused by simple, practical things. One of the most common causes of test anxiety is that a person does not feel adequately prepared for their test. This feeling can be the result of many different issues such as poor study habits or lack of organization, but the most common culprit is time management. Starting to study too late, failing to organize your study time to cover all of the material, or being distracted while you study will mean that you're not well prepared for the test. This may lead to cramming the night before, which will cause you to be physically and mentally exhausted for the test. Poor time management also contributes to feelings of stress, fear, and hopelessness as you realize you are not well prepared but don't know what to do about it.

Other times, test anxiety is not related to your preparation for the test but comes from unresolved fear. This may be a past failure on a test, or poor performance on tests in general. It may come from comparing yourself to others who seem to be performing better or from the stress of living up to expectations. Anxiety may be driven by fears of the future—how failure on this test would affect your educational and career goals. These fears are often completely irrational, but they can still negatively impact your test performance.

> **Review Video: 3 Reasons You Have Test Anxiety**
> Visit mometrix.com/academy and enter code: 428468

Elements of Test Anxiety

As mentioned earlier, test anxiety is considered to be an emotional state, but it has physical and mental components as well. Sometimes you may not even realize that you are suffering from test anxiety until you notice the physical symptoms. These can include trembling hands, rapid heartbeat, sweating, nausea, and tense muscles. Extreme anxiety may lead to fainting or vomiting. Obviously, any of these symptoms can have a negative impact on testing. It is important to recognize them as soon as they begin to occur so that you can address the problem before it damages your performance.

> **Review Video: 3 Ways to Tell You Have Test Anxiety**
> Visit mometrix.com/academy and enter code: 927847

The mental components of test anxiety include trouble focusing and inability to remember learned information. During a test, your mind is on high alert, which can help you recall information and stay focused for an extended period of time. However, anxiety interferes with your mind's natural processes, causing you to blank out, even on the questions you know well. The strain of testing during anxiety makes it difficult to stay focused, especially on a test that may take several hours. Extreme anxiety can take a huge mental toll, making it difficult not only to recall test information but even to understand the test questions or pull your thoughts together.

> **Review Video: How Test Anxiety Affects Memory**
> Visit mometrix.com/academy and enter code: 609003

Effects of Test Anxiety

Test anxiety is like a disease—if left untreated, it will get progressively worse. Anxiety leads to poor performance, and this reinforces the feelings of fear and failure, which in turn lead to poor performances on subsequent tests. It can grow from a mild nervousness to a crippling condition. If allowed to progress, test anxiety can have a big impact on your schooling, and consequently on your future.

Test anxiety can spread to other parts of your life. Anxiety on tests can become anxiety in any stressful situation, and blanking on a test can turn into panicking in a job situation. But fortunately, you don't have to let anxiety rule your testing and determine your grades. There are a number of relatively simple steps you can take to move past anxiety and function normally on a test and in the rest of life.

> **Review Video: How Test Anxiety Impacts Your Grades**
> Visit mometrix.com/academy and enter code: 939819

Physical Steps for Beating Test Anxiety

While test anxiety is a serious problem, the good news is that it can be overcome. It doesn't have to control your ability to think and remember information. While it may take time, you can begin taking steps today to beat anxiety.

Just as your first hint that you may be struggling with anxiety comes from the physical symptoms, the first step to treating it is also physical. Rest is crucial for having a clear, strong mind. If you are tired, it is much easier to give in to anxiety. But if you establish good sleep habits, your body and mind will be ready to perform optimally, without the strain of exhaustion. Additionally, sleeping well helps you to retain information better, so you're more likely to recall the answers when you see the test questions.

Getting good sleep means more than going to bed on time. It's important to allow your brain time to relax. Take study breaks from time to time so it doesn't get overworked, and don't study right before bed. Take time to rest your mind before trying to rest your body, or you may find it difficult to fall asleep.

> **Review Video: The Importance of Sleep for Your Brain**
> Visit mometrix.com/academy and enter code: 319338

Along with sleep, other aspects of physical health are important in preparing for a test. Good nutrition is vital for good brain function. Sugary foods and drinks may give a burst of energy but this burst is followed by a crash, both physically and emotionally. Instead, fuel your body with protein and vitamin-rich foods.

Also, drink plenty of water. Dehydration can lead to headaches and exhaustion, especially if your brain is already under stress from the rigors of the test. Particularly if your test is a long one, drink water during the breaks. And if possible, take an energy-boosting snack to eat between sections.

> **Review Video: How Diet Can Affect your Mood**
> Visit mometrix.com/academy and enter code: 624317

Along with sleep and diet, a third important part of physical health is exercise. Maintaining a steady workout schedule is helpful, but even taking 5-minute study breaks to walk can help get your blood pumping faster and clear your head. Exercise also releases endorphins, which contribute to a positive feeling and can help combat test anxiety.

When you nurture your physical health, you are also contributing to your mental health. If your body is healthy, your mind is much more likely to be healthy as well. So take time to rest, nourish your body with healthy food and water, and get moving as much as possible. Taking these physical steps will make you stronger and more able to take the mental steps necessary to overcome test anxiety.

Mental Steps for Beating Test Anxiety

Working on the mental side of test anxiety can be more challenging, but as with the physical side, there are clear steps you can take to overcome it. As mentioned earlier, test anxiety often stems from lack of preparation, so the obvious solution is to prepare for the test. Effective studying may be the most important weapon you have for beating test anxiety, but you can and should employ several other mental tools to combat fear.

First, boost your confidence by reminding yourself of past success—tests or projects that you aced. If you're putting as much effort into preparing for this test as you did for those, there's no reason you should expect to fail here. Work hard to prepare; then trust your preparation.

Second, surround yourself with encouraging people. It can be helpful to find a study group, but be sure that the people you're around will encourage a positive attitude. If you spend time with others who are anxious or cynical, this will only contribute to your own anxiety. Look for others who are motivated to study hard from a desire to succeed, not from a fear of failure.

Third, reward yourself. A test is physically and mentally tiring, even without anxiety, and it can be helpful to have something to look forward to. Plan an activity following the test, regardless of the outcome, such as going to a movie or getting ice cream.

When you are taking the test, if you find yourself beginning to feel anxious, remind yourself that you know the material. Visualize successfully completing the test. Then take a few deep, relaxing breaths and return to it. Work through the questions carefully but with confidence, knowing that you are capable of succeeding.

Developing a healthy mental approach to test taking will also aid in other areas of life. Test anxiety affects more than just the actual test—it can be damaging to your mental health and even contribute to depression. It's important to beat test anxiety before it becomes a problem for more than testing.

> **Review Video: Test Anxiety and Depression**
> Visit mometrix.com/academy and enter code: 904704

Study Strategy

Being prepared for the test is necessary to combat anxiety, but what does being prepared look like? You may study for hours on end and still not feel prepared. What you need is a strategy for test prep. The next few pages outline our recommended steps to help you plan out and conquer the challenge of preparation.

STEP 1: SCOPE OUT THE TEST

Learn everything you can about the format (multiple choice, essay, etc.) and what will be on the test. Gather any study materials, course outlines, or sample exams that may be available. Not only will this help you to prepare, but knowing what to expect can help to alleviate test anxiety.

STEP 2: MAP OUT THE MATERIAL

Look through the textbook or study guide and make note of how many chapters or sections it has. Then divide these over the time you have. For example, if a book has 15 chapters and you have five days to study, you need to cover three chapters each day. Even better, if you have the time, leave an extra day at the end for overall review after you have gone through the material in depth.

If time is limited, you may need to prioritize the material. Look through it and make note of which sections you think you already have a good grasp on, and which need review. While you are studying, skim quickly through the familiar sections and take more time on the challenging parts. Write out your plan so you don't get lost as you go. Having a written plan also helps you feel more in control of the study, so anxiety is less likely to arise from feeling overwhelmed at the amount to cover.

STEP 3: GATHER YOUR TOOLS

Decide what study method works best for you. Do you prefer to highlight in the book as you study and then go back over the highlighted portions? Or do you type out notes of the important information? Or is it helpful to make flashcards that you can carry with you? Assemble the pens, index cards, highlighters, post-it notes, and any other materials you may need so you won't be distracted by getting up to find things while you study.

If you're having a hard time retaining the information or organizing your notes, experiment with different methods. For example, try color-coding by subject with colored pens, highlighters, or post-it notes. If you learn better by hearing, try recording yourself reading your notes so you can listen while in the car, working out, or simply sitting at your desk. Ask a friend to quiz you from your flashcards, or try teaching someone the material to solidify it in your mind.

STEP 4: CREATE YOUR ENVIRONMENT

It's important to avoid distractions while you study. This includes both the obvious distractions like visitors and the subtle distractions like an uncomfortable chair (or a too-comfortable couch that makes you want to fall asleep). Set up the best study environment possible: good lighting and a comfortable work area. If background music helps you focus, you may want to turn it on, but otherwise keep the room quiet. If you are using a computer to take notes, be sure you don't have any other windows open, especially applications like social media, games, or anything else that could distract you. Silence your phone and turn off notifications. Be sure to keep water close by so you stay hydrated while you study (but avoid unhealthy drinks and snacks).

Also, take into account the best time of day to study. Are you freshest first thing in the morning? Try to set aside some time then to work through the material. Is your mind clearer in the afternoon or evening? Schedule your study session then. Another method is to study at the same time of day that you will take the test, so that your brain gets used to working on the material at that time and will be ready to focus at test time.

STEP 5: STUDY!

Once you have done all the study preparation, it's time to settle into the actual studying. Sit down, take a few moments to settle your mind so you can focus, and begin to follow your study plan. Don't give in to distractions or let yourself procrastinate. This is your time to prepare so you'll be ready to fearlessly approach the test. Make the most of the time and stay focused.

Of course, you don't want to burn out. If you study too long you may find that you're not retaining the information very well. Take regular study breaks. For example, taking five minutes out of every hour to walk briskly, breathing deeply and swinging your arms, can help your mind stay fresh.

As you get to the end of each chapter or section, it's a good idea to do a quick review. Remind yourself of what you learned and work on any difficult parts. When you feel that you've mastered the material, move on to the next part. At the end of your study session, briefly skim through your notes again.

But while review is helpful, cramming last minute is NOT. If at all possible, work ahead so that you won't need to fit all your study into the last day. Cramming overloads your brain with more information than it can process and retain, and your tired mind may struggle to recall even previously learned information when it is overwhelmed with last-minute study. Also, the urgent nature of cramming and the stress placed on your brain contribute to anxiety. You'll be more likely to go to the test feeling unprepared and having trouble thinking clearly.

So don't cram, and don't stay up late before the test, even just to review your notes at a leisurely pace. Your brain needs rest more than it needs to go over the information again. In fact, plan to finish your studies by noon or early afternoon the day before the test. Give your brain the rest of the day to relax or focus on other things, and get a good night's sleep. Then you will be fresh for the test and better able to recall what you've studied.

STEP 6: TAKE A PRACTICE TEST

Many courses offer sample tests, either online or in the study materials. This is an excellent resource to check whether you have mastered the material, as well as to prepare for the test format and environment.

Check the test format ahead of time: the number of questions, the type (multiple choice, free response, etc.), and the time limit. Then create a plan for working through them. For example, if you have 30 minutes to take a 60-question test, your limit is 30 seconds per question. Spend less time on the questions you know well so that you can take more time on the difficult ones.

If you have time to take several practice tests, take the first one open book, with no time limit. Work through the questions at your own pace and make sure you fully understand them. Gradually work up to taking a test under test conditions: sit at a desk with all study materials put away and set a timer. Pace yourself to make sure you finish the test with time to spare and go back to check your answers if you have time.

After each test, check your answers. On the questions you missed, be sure you understand why you missed them. Did you misread the question (tests can use tricky wording)? Did you forget the information? Or was it something you hadn't learned? Go back and study any shaky areas that the practice tests reveal.

Taking these tests not only helps with your grade, but also aids in combating test anxiety. If you're already used to the test conditions, you're less likely to worry about it, and working through tests until you're scoring well gives you a confidence boost. Go through the practice tests until you feel comfortable, and then you can go into the test knowing that you're ready for it.

Test Tips

On test day, you should be confident, knowing that you've prepared well and are ready to answer the questions. But aside from preparation, there are several test day strategies you can employ to maximize your performance.

First, as stated before, get a good night's sleep the night before the test (and for several nights before that, if possible). Go into the test with a fresh, alert mind rather than staying up late to study.

Try not to change too much about your normal routine on the day of the test. It's important to eat a nutritious breakfast, but if you normally don't eat breakfast at all, consider eating just a protein bar. If you're a coffee drinker, go ahead and have your normal coffee. Just make sure you time it so that the caffeine doesn't wear off right in the middle of your test. Avoid sugary beverages, and drink enough water to stay hydrated but not so much that you need a restroom break 10 minutes into the test. If your test isn't first thing in the morning, consider going for a walk or doing a light workout before the test to get your blood flowing.

Allow yourself enough time to get ready, and leave for the test with plenty of time to spare so you won't have the anxiety of scrambling to arrive in time. Another reason to be early is to select a good seat. It's helpful to sit away from doors and windows, which can be distracting. Find a good seat, get out your supplies, and settle your mind before the test begins.

When the test begins, start by going over the instructions carefully, even if you already know what to expect. Make sure you avoid any careless mistakes by following the directions.

Then begin working through the questions, pacing yourself as you've practiced. If you're not sure on an answer, don't spend too much time on it, and don't let it shake your confidence. Either skip it and come back later, or eliminate as many wrong answers as possible and guess among the remaining ones. Don't dwell on these questions as you continue—put them out of your mind and focus on what lies ahead.

Be sure to read all of the answer choices, even if you're sure the first one is the right answer. Sometimes you'll find a better one if you keep reading. But don't second-guess yourself if you do immediately know the answer. Your gut instinct is usually right. Don't let test anxiety rob you of the information you know.

If you have time at the end of the test (and if the test format allows), go back and review your answers. Be cautious about changing any, since your first instinct tends to be correct, but make sure you didn't misread any of the questions or accidentally mark the wrong answer choice. Look over any you skipped and make an educated guess.

At the end, leave the test feeling confident. You've done your best, so don't waste time worrying about your performance or wishing you could change anything. Instead, celebrate the successful completion of this test. And finally, use this test to learn how to deal with anxiety even better next time.

> **Review Video: 5 Tips to Beat Test Anxiety**
> Visit mometrix.com/academy and enter code: 570656

Important Qualification

Not all anxiety is created equal. If your test anxiety is causing major issues in your life beyond the classroom or testing center, or if you are experiencing troubling physical symptoms related to your anxiety, it may be a sign of a serious physiological or psychological condition. If this sounds like your situation, we strongly encourage you to seek professional help.

Tell Us Your Story

We at Mometrix would like to extend our heartfelt thanks to you for letting us be a part of your journey. It is an honor to serve people from all walks of life, people like you, who are committed to building the best future they can for themselves.

We know that each person's situation is unique. But we also know that, whether you are a young student or a mother of four, you care about working to make your own life and the lives of those around you better.

That's why we want to hear your story.

We want to know why you're taking this test. We want to know about the trials you've gone through to get here. And we want to know about the successes you've experienced after taking and passing your test.

In addition to your story, which can be an inspiration both to us and to others, we value your feedback. We want to know both what you loved about our book and what you think we can improve on.

The team at Mometrix would be absolutely thrilled to hear from you!
So please, send us an email at tellusyourstory@mometrix.com or visit us at mometrix.com/tellusyourstory.php and let's stay in touch.

Made in the USA
Las Vegas, NV
21 May 2023